When the Ghosts Come Ashore

When the Ghosts Come Ashore

Jacqui Germain

Button Poetry / Exploding Pinecone Press
Minneapolis, Minnesota
2016

Published by Button Poetry / Exploding Pinecone Press
Minneapolis, MN 55403

http://buttonpoetry.com

Manufactured in the United States of America

Cover Image: Brianna McCarthy
Cover Design: Doug Paul Case | | dougpaulcase@gmail.com

ISBN 978-1-943735-05-1

TABLE OF CONTENTS

SANKOFA

I wrote a poem once abo ut
black boys disappearing right
out of the   like a shut

mouth   a   stream
of   bullets right down
its throat. All of t heir   black

boy eyes lik e   b l a c k
rocks staring at me right off
the page like they wouldn't

sink if I dropped them all
in a   r i v e r. And I wonder if
it's healthy to keep all these

ghosts in my pocket. All their
hands that   you can't
see   but   they push

things around when you
                              aren't
even looking. What the body

becomes when it carries you and them.
How your bones n e g o t i a t e
weight and   weightless,

learn to manage the absence
and the homecoming in every
reunion. We black folks who bend

words, folks who celebrate the ghosts
that show up in our poems
like a

3

shout or sometimes   a
sweep of wind   that   carries   you

all the way to a tree branch
or a potter's field or the bottom
          of

          the   Atlantic
my   g   o   d   it's   crowded

down
h   e   r   e
like

y
o
u

wouldn't believe. And I wonder
if it's healthy to h a v e   them
                    all sitting in my

                              or my
     or eating dinner   r i g h t
                    next to my elbow

          like they always knew
          t h e y   w o u l d   f i n d
               a home   here.

BLOOD

I build a revolution
in my bedroom
every time I masturbate.

My own body conspires
to assassinate both
my rebel hands.

No matter
what I do, my history
still tells itself wrong.

My lips shape both
casualties and
freedom songs, but

I still have sex like
the dogs won't bite if you
have your church shoes on,

like black Grandmas didn't
keep all their shotguns
up underneath a mattress.

FOR YEARS, THE ONLY THING I KNEW TO COMPARE MY SKIN TO WAS DIRT

after the painting "In All (For You and I)" by Brianna McCarthy

Girls, with all their blk
skin and their blk
hair and their blk
eyes, got these bright orange kidneys,
these clementine-colored lumps of flesh,
got these blue-striped mountains
wrapped around their foreheads,
these tall, tall trees with grapefruit,
with grapefruit-blood leaves
draped down the front of their noses.

Girls, with all their blk
armpits and their blk
elbows and their blk
areolas, got these green and gold patterned breastplates
carved right under their skin, right above their ribs,
glowing just underneath all that blk, blk, blk.

Girls, with all their blk
shadows and their blk
ears hearing blk
things and their knees bending into blk
things and their blk
spines twisting and curving and holding and lifting all this blk-
ness, got these long bowing, bending necks
with yellow spiked arms coming out of them,
and purple jagged teeth coming out the top
and long turquoise legs coming out the bottom.

THE ATLANTIC AS IT WELCOMES THE GHOSTS

The blue ocean is a wrist snatched back.
The blue ocean is a broken arm flapping back against the shore.
The blue ocean is a twisted elbow
trying to remember what its shoulder feels like.
The blue ocean is a red, slapped cheek
rippling with nausea and shock,
seeping blood from its gums,
tasting every name of every black body
tossed over the edge of every ship,
every letter stuck between the ocean's teeth,
all their bones collecting beneath its tongue
like a basket of sour fruit.

The welcome is a blue tongue pressed
between sand and black teeth,
seething at the wooden ships scraping across its back,
flower-petal-ing black bodies in their drooling wake.
The welcome is the sun baking the blue surface,
boiling the ocean water til the bones are clean,
letting the spirits shift up out of their terror
and rise with the waves like steam.
Dead black folk flying away look just like exhale,
a warm sunlight ascension above a field of waves.

But the bones stay & keep house
& make home below the shore &
here, the steam comes back to sleep.

ST. LOUIS

after Aziza Barnes

So I walk into a bar, right?
And everyone is dancing to their own
kind of liquor and beat
and that's when I spot her,
St. Louis, sitting at a corner stool
drinking Schlafly and watching the scene.

And my friend says, *Yo, St. Louis!*
Yo, Chicago-knock-off city!
Yo, Midwest-Mississippi-forgotten!
Yo, empty bucket, clogged-gutter skyline!

St. Louis looks over at us,
and turns into a whole role of caution tape,

and my friend goes,
Yo, you blues'-bastard-child-singing-in-the-wrong-key!
Yo, you public-housing-graveyard-in-cheap-makeup city!
Yo, you gateway, archway, the biggest, bloodiest wide open exit wound!

The whole bar gets the joke.
St. Louis is not even a bullet,
just the empty space that's left.
The bar's laughter fills the hollow finger
of burning air and stuffs the wound with noise.
The room is full of wet lips and big teeth and thick smoke
and I swear, I feel like shit.

I walk towards her offering a fresh beer
and a Sunday morning's worth of apologies.
St. Louis looks at me like the whole East side
has gone up in flames. Again. And I realize
I have brought the city a peace gift of lighter fluid
instead of water. I want to say,

I know you. I've been to East St. Louis, I know
about the race riots. I know about the failed
housing projects downtown, I watched a documentary.
I read a book about the foreclosure crisis.
I understand that poverty is two hands
clamped over an entire neighborhood. I get that
this is how you are fitted for handcuffs. Please.
Don't act like you don't know me. I'm trying to help you.
I've read the books. I wrote a paper on it.
I know what Delmar looks like without the students there.
I've walked through the North side and seen the buildings
with only gums left. I know parts of you have only gums left.

St. Louis is the Mississippi riverbank and she
looks at me like I am the clumsy ship run aground in her thigh,
trying desperately to make peace with the mud.

She says to me, *I have seen you before.*
You have "University" around your neck,
though you wear all my things.
You have washed in the river and still smell of bleach.
They have taught you how to make molds of my mouth
in plaster, but not how to let me speak.
You use my bones as fodder in the classroom
and ask nothing of my flesh.
Even now, you pity my silence.
You think I cannot speak,
but I just choose not to speak to you.
I do not know what little you have learned
of my name, but I have known yours for a century.
I recognized the tower before it was built.

We always do.

THE HARVEST

If I were to die
in police custody,
their handcuffs would
be my ex-lover's
mouth, my ex-lover's mouth
would be a series
of teeth, the teeth rows
of enamel fingers digging
into my flesh, my flesh be a plot
of land, the plot of land
would be a map of bleeding
artifacts, the bleeding
be place-markers
for buried collarbones,
the buried seedlings, collarbones
the white men planted,
the seedlings the white men
planted be the ghosts
that call for the plow,
the plow the fist that pulls
the harvest, the harvest the coffee shop
selling a Columbian village
for $6 a cup, the harvest a history
textbook falling asleep on itself in class,
a Walgreens on every corner, the harvest
every city we pretend the *Dream*

survives in

                the harvest is their *Dream* rotting,

                    the harvest is every
                    Walgreens decaying
                    with flame & smashed
                    windows, is a bankrupt
                    & rotting classroom,
                    is burnt & rotting coffee,

is rotted teeth, is sick
& green with
the harvest's gifts
refusing the tongue,
to feed the body that
consumes it, is the whole
land spoiling itself to kill
the fingers that dug it raw,
the white teeth, the wide
eyes, the blue badge
that saw me & whistled,

*Shit. Look at her. I bet she
tastes too sweet.*

HOW AMERICA LOVES FERGUSON TWEETS MORE THAN THE CITY OF FERGUSON (OR ANY OF THE EIGHTY-NINE OTHER MUNICIPALITIES IN ST. LOUIS)

The camera-flash séance
in the middle of West Florissant

searches for ghosts
in the street lamps,

while black bodies mid-funeral,
caped in tear gas

contort into résumé
bullet points.

Our jaws broke open
in grief make front page

in an article that doesn't mention
St. Louis, but will

win an award for how the photo
makes taxidermy of our trauma.

Thank god for the internet,
how we've taught ourselves

to play mortician with each
new name we are given,

to pinpoint a single
faulty organ, mistake it

for the whole body,
neglect to even ask

the bones for a name.
Thank god for twitter,

for the microphones
and media equipment,

for the scavengers' descent
onto a single street,

for how they ate
our terror and vomited

a news story,
for the blossoming

of our messy grief
on television screens

for a few weeks.

ROTTED FRUIT

Somewhere, in some city in Kentucky,
my brother is sitting in his apartment.
I do not know what color the carpet is.
I have no idea how his furniture is arranged.
The year my brother stopped speaking to me,
I lost my own name in the shower.
I began looking for it in the mouths
of people who did not care to spell it correctly.
I had not yet learned how to retrieve it.
I watched each letter cleave to their molars,
spoil, stink, become the thing to wash out.
This is how I learned to give my name away,
to apologize in cursive for the first thing
my mother gave me
that wasn't her own blood.

Somewhere in some city south of Cincinnati,
my brother is sitting in his apartment.
I do not know what his kitchen cupboards look like.
I have no idea what wall his TV is on.
The year my brother's face became a shut door,
I grew two extra fists along my spine
and made a list of all the things
I had left on his doorstep.
I stopped knocking. I traveled west.
I spoke of my brother like a lost language,
only said his name when the wind was just right
and I knew it would carry the sound elsewhere.
I found my name on the third floor of a dorm
and buried his beneath the building.
I rode my spine home every holiday
and returned only with a string of knuckles.
My parents spoke of the fingers as if they were
not curled. My brother did not
speak at all. He never even
brought his hands home.

Somewhere east of St. Louis,
my brother is sitting in his apartment.
I have not seen it. I do not want to.
I imagine his name has dug itself up by now,
has finally gone back home. I have not
said it aloud in years. My mouth is not a fist
but neither is it an open palm.
I have no taste for rotted fruit.
I do not imagine his hands.
They are not mine to peel open.

QUESTIONS FOR THE WOMAN I WAS LAST NIGHT, 1

after Kush Thompson, after Warsan Shire

When you picked apart the white of his knuckles
to see if his white was different from all the other
white, did the black girl ghosts scare you?

When you closed his palms and his lips
closed your throat, did you see the audience
of dark shoulders sitting by the stairs?

When you sighed under the white crows of his supple
fingers feasting in a flurry below your chest,
did your moan lullaby the dead black girls to sleep?

Once they were asleep, did his teeth
feel like maybe they could pop your black
open and tongue it off your bones?

How soon afterwards did you fall off the bed
and begin writhing on the carpet? Did this man
stand over you watching your spasm?

How quickly did your swimming arms wrap
around his ankles? Remind you of an altar quaking
beneath the weight of all that fresh sin?

Did your arms wrapped around his ankles
make you feel *maybe* like a sexy wet dream
white boys tuck beneath their dicks?

Did your arms wrapped around his ankles
suddenly give the false idol a face and a neck
that laughed at your lust?

How quickly does this positioning betray?
How quickly do his ankles betray? His grin
betray? How black girl do you feel?

How quickly does your back
on the carpet scratch
or soften your peeling spine?

How soon does your flesh
de-bone itself, does your black
cough out its own teeth?

NAT TURNER GOES VACATIONING IN D.C.

The city is quiet and completely empty.
Nat Turner takes his shoes off,
walks down the middle of the road,
and follows the yellow double line to the heart of the city.

He presses his toes into the tar,
tries to feel the blood pulsing below the surface.
He follows the river downtown.
He follows the river to the MLK memorial,

applies his palms to the base.
The stone feels cold, memory-less
despite the carved quotes, blood-less
despite the protruding body.

He climbs to the top of the monument,
leans into the sunset and raises his ax above his head,
throws his shoulders down into the rock
and chips the corner of King's hand.

He thinks it's funny, that we took a rock
and tried to pull a body out of it,
called it *honor*, named it *memory*.
He leans again, ax above his head, shoulders—

and again, chips a bit of granite away.
Again and again until Nat hollows out a hole.
He squeezes the handle, kisses the metal,
drops the ax into the chiseled spot.

Hours later, the sun slowly rises.
An outline of a black man with an ax
spreads onto the grass.
Nat turns his back on the monument.

There is nothing in memory but a mouth-less shadow.
He follows the river of blood back down the road,
leaves the city-state full of stone
and carved quotes, empty of bodies and memory,

full of so many shadows and so many ghosts.

HOW AMERICA LOVES CHICAGO'S GHOSTS MORE THAN THE PEOPLE STILL LIVING IN THE CITY

an erasure of Chance The Rapper's "Paranoia"

Eyes been on the gun,

on the dying,

the shit neighborhood.

They watch the paper,

watch the hood boy militia

trapped in the middle of the sun.

Lips with a lotta murder talk.

They probably scared of all the

dark dark down here. Our nation,

dry eyes, paranoia and a lotta dying,

been pouring fireworks in the summer.

I hear everybody's god

a little scared too.

QUESTIONS FOR THE WOMAN I WAS LAST NIGHT, 3

after Kush Thompson, after Warsan Shire

How are you still unable to make
your pelvis a bible? How do you become
a glutton for pain and still blame
the dinner plate for being full?

How do you substitute addiction
for addiction for giving up
your history in shame's mouth?
How is your mouth a city lost

beneath the sea and really just
a wet grave at the same time?
Is your mouth really just a mass
burial for the burning sheets?

Will the burning sheets
become your body's swaddling
clothes, damp with moving flesh?
Will you arise come morning?

Do your hands push through
the fabric like stretched skin?
Do you fight it? Do you ever
fight or does the smoke calm you?

When you wake up smelling
like a burnt house, melted plastic
and appliances, do you
tell yourself you will rebuild?

CONJURING: A LESSON IN WORDS AND GHOSTS

Our desks are in a circle in our classroom & it just so happens I'm sitting next to my white professor & all my black girl hair is flung over one shoulder & I can see everyone's face & my professor, we're talking about the 1920s & my professor, he says *nigger* & before that we were talking about Ralph Ellison & before that we were talking about Claude McKay & we skipped over Nella Larson & made fun of Gwendolyn a bit, but c'est la vie & my professor, he runs right through *nigger* like it's not a wall my whole history is pinned up against & *nigger* sits in the middle of all of our desks & it's like I'm the only one who can see it & everyone else in the room turns white even though they're not; they're pink & pale & sandy & tree-colored but still, everyone I mean everything turns white & I'm just a dot & I'm just a black girl with black girl hair & my black girl hips balanced in this dark red chair & we all know *nigger* is tree-colored & I can't remember my face & my tongue bleeds right into my teeth & my mouth is full of spit & he didn't mean it that way & this is academia & here comes the whole train of them, right? & don't tell me I can't say that word but you can & be mature / professional / quiet / good & freedom of speech & here they come & here's the list of their freedoms they fight for but what about mine & I'm being honest, he really didn't mean it that way & it's just a word & my tongue & my teeth & language is such a complicated series of ropes and ladders & black folk be climbing and hanging at the same time & he only read it in context & it's in the context of the reading & it's in the reading & we all know *nigger* is tree-colored, which is to say, we all know *nigger* has black people hanging off the g's, which is to say, some words carry ghosts no matter what because context & context is everything & my professor is talking about & is talking about & is talking about & is talking about & is talking about & is talking about & is talking about & just like that, the whole room is haunted.

HOW THE ATLANTIC OCEAN PREPARES FOR WAR

The Atlantic is a map of bones.
The Atlantic is a mouth of ancient boulders.
The Atlantic is holding massacre
like a keepsake against its heart.

The Atlantic is painting the sunset in blood
just above its receding hairline.
The Atlantic is stuffing its pockets
with photographs of children.

The Atlantic is drunk on Motown.
The Atlantic is drunk on jazz so black
its blue because
after things are black for a long time
they become blue.

The Atlantic has my jaw in its fist because my teeth
and tongue have curled into knuckles.
The Atlantic has Africa in its fist
because they've been trading ghosts for centuries.

The Atlantic has Haiti in its fist
because the slaves had so much fight
it filled up the moon;
the moon moves everything.

The Atlantic has fists where
its knees should be.
The Atlantic has fists where
its shoulders curl into arms.
The Atlantic has fists where
its waist is supposed to bend.

The Atlantic punches everything,
has fists where its eye sockets
punch back at the gaping holes in the moon,
collide, caress, call each other family.

THE SPLIT ROCK PRAYS TO WHATEVER BROKE IT

Rage is not to be avoided, diminished, belittled. Rage is God. Better believe my rage is seeped in love. – Shira Erlichman

Let my anger be warm and ripe with love.
Let it reek of car crashes that we have all survived.
Let it breathe. Let it dance in my fists.
Let it collapse drunk and merry
across my knees, my bedspread.
Let my anger be a thick, bubbling bath
and the cool towel by the windowsill.
Let my anger stretch into a generous wingspan.
Let it be a split rock, a steady hammer,
a plank of wood that still remembers the whole tree.
Let it sweeten the milk, turn the mug steaming
hot against the freezing chatter in my teeth.
Let it be thick thick as a St. Louis summer.
Let it be thick and just as full of memory
and just as full of arched backs stretching the tired
out of their spines, and just as full of black,
and just as full of blues.
Let my anger be the city of St. Louis, fresh-faced,
looking in the mirror at all its pimples and stretch marks,
looking at all its hard beauty that belongs to itself only,
calling up Detroit, calling up Philly and all those cities saying,
Baby, let's all go dancing. Let's roll our windows down and sing.
Bring all your busted windows and overgrown lawns
and new coffee shops we can't afford and the schools
closing or not and the naked empty lots and cellulite sidewalks
and bring all your dead musicians and we'll make a night of it.
Let my anger be the celebration we were never
supposed to have because we were never
supposed to know we had anything
worth celebrating.

QUENTIN TARANTINO OR WHY I DO NOT TRUST YOU WITH MY HISTORY OR ON WEARING A GAUDY ROBE WHILE GRABBING THE ASS OF A NAKED BLACK WOMAN FOR A MAGAZINE

I picture you mostly
as an arrangement of limbs.
You are the tenderest butcher.
All of you is eyes up-
and-down-ing my frame.
All of you is hands, knuckles
pounding out a drumbeat.
All of you is mining my throat
for gold with your fingers.
All of you fingerprints, birthmarks.
All of you is fingers like stretch marks.

Mama said keep your hands to yourself

All of you dancing on broken back.
All of you the biggest hands,
say you just want to touch me.

Mama said keep your hands

All of you is eyelids and eyes.
All of you is mouth
kissing your nameplate
in the nestled home between my breasts,
licking the tree branch of my collarbone,
tripping over the notches of each noose,
drooling down the river of my spine.
You are the tenderest butcher.
Just want to squeeze me.
Just want to touch it

Mama said

All of you is spit

Mama said

All of you tongue snake
all the way around my throat.
All of you thin pink wire lips,
All of you such big hands
touching everything,

    Mama said keep your hands

All of you
butcher
stench
think you own
everything, think
you own *my*
everything.
All of you
grin
laugh
lean back
cock your head
suck your teeth
toothpick my *black*
pinky-finger-pick
me out your
mouth like a snapped neck bone

      be   careful   cuz
      Mama   said
      I   can   still   choke   you

All of you
such big mouth,
so many teeth.

I always picture you
bloated, freshly-feasted,
your dinner plate,
a gravestone,
bones picked clean.

THINGS I SHOULD SAY TO MYSELF IN THE MIRROR OR THINGS I WOULD SAY TO THE CITY OF ST.LOUIS IF IT COULD HEAR ME

I've been planning
to leave you for years.
It began as a quiet urging
in the bottom of my heels
and now I dream
only of highways.
My desk drawer
opens to the smell
of engine exhaust
and the letter I wrote
when I was nineteen
and made my wrists
a cave of plane tickets.

It is a sign of prudent planning
to have marked an escape route
through your own bones.

Once, after all the policemen
left your forearm,
I walked my eyes along
the scar tissue on Delmar,
pretending, casually,
that I was your lover.
I did it nearly every day
for a whole summer
until I couldn't help
but smell entirely of skin.

Don't be so hard
on yourself. Half of you
is postcard, while the other
half of you is trying

29

to rebuild what, years ago,
was burned to the ground
by someone else. You are
always rebuilding. You are
always reaching for the river.

You have survived so much
that no one remembers.
And you still spread warm
rain on all your overgrown
lots. And you still get dressed
in the morning. You still
open wide for the sun.

NAT TURNER FINDS OUT I'M CONSIDERING NOT GOING BACK TO SCHOOL TO FINISH MY UNDERGRADUATE DEGREE

I'm at a table by the wall,
hugging a small coffee with both hands.

Nat walks into the nutmeg-filled shop,
lays a wrinkled hand on my shoulder.

I stand, breathless; we exit the diner together.
Outside on the sidewalk, under the grey sky,

I lean into his heavy shadow.
I am drunk on the gravity of his bones.

He holds my hand as we walk and instantly I am
eleven years old. I want nothing more than to

hear him speak. His lips, a mountain-range above
his chin. We walk this way: two matches, one lit,

down the street until we arrive at a cemetery.
We walk to the center of the gated field. He presses his

hand against my cheek. I feel no heartbeat
but his skin is buzzing. The sky rolls into dusk.

He slaps me.   Hard.   Surrounded in tombstones.
Says first,   *"Some of us ain't even got no rock."*

My whole face is hot. He presses his hand against my
cheek. I smell blood. I begin to cry. I'm so sorry.

He touches my shoulder. He kisses my forehead.
He drags his thumb under each eye, brushes away the water

& the salt. The humid air leaves sweat above his eyebrows.
I continue to cry. From my lip, I taste that I am leaking blood.

Says second, *"Our people know these two things best:*
            water and salt.   We cry when we run out of sweat,
                        we sweat when we tired of cry."

Nat, sweating. Me, cheek burning, still crying.
Both of us, surrounded by rocks and ghosts.

For an hour we stay gathered here, buried in fog.
I stop crying. We make eye contact for the first time.

Says last, *"Good. You tired of cry. Now go back to school,*
                                    and sweat."

BIPOLAR IS BORED AND RENAMES ITSELF

I have recently come to the realization
that I will be writing "the bipolar disorder poem"
for the rest of my life.
                        There are hundreds of ways
to say *I am wrapped in my own bees' nest.*
or *My body is a haunted*
        house that I am lost in.
        There are no doors but there are knives
        and a hundred windows.
or *My body has apologized*
        to my body.
        My body is not
        sure if it accepts.
or *I am a river with*
        a dam at its neck
        that has begun
        to drown its own fish.
or *I am a field setting itself on fire*
        just to become the sun.
or *I am a newborn so obsessed*
        with the birth,
        I throttle my own throat
        and hope for a repeat.
or *I am a ball of melted wax*
        burying my own wick.
or *I am the flame*
        melting my body
        down into a hard mess.
or *My eyes have learned not to believe themselves.*
or *My eyes have learned the sky will be*
        a red sea of winged teeth if you believe it to be so.
or *I am trapped behind eyes*
        that recognize the demon in everything.
or *There is a demon in everything;*
        I know this.
or *My brain is my own cracked windshield,*

my own bug-splattered glass mirror
and I am driving towards the sunrise.
or *I am still driving*
 towards the sunrise.

SILK

On this night, my body
unwound like a spool.
I was beneath a boy
who loved thread for all the things
he could make of it.

Tonight, I am smooth and pliable
like good silk before a snag.
I am a metaphor for anything
beautiful and ruin-able when it
hooks on to sharp things.

He lays his full weight
on my torso and I am a leaf
pressed still onto the mattress,
pressed small and flat by something living
for the purpose of study.

I am not sad about this.
It's here that I can feel all my edges,
visualize my outline best
against a hungry white backdrop.
I am not sad about this.

I am dry despite the spit
and I am dry despite the fire hydrant
opening along the sidewalk of my spine,
giving my dancing vertebrae reprieve
in such repressive heat.

Beneath the grunting face
of the simplest kind of sex,
when two people want things
that are not each other, so settle
for a drive-thru buffet of each other's lips—

It's okay. I am dry and sort of shiny
but dull on the other side
like good silk.

/ /

I don't really remember the snagging
but at some point he stops
and looks down at our axis
to find blood.

I gave him a fake name
when we met, so I feel like
maybe the red is someone else's
admission of guilt, a red slap

on my ass that melted into shame,
a kiss so hard and hungry
it poured its color onto the sheets
or maybe the fire hydrant's water

ran out of blue and started
spraying out its own red self
from my opening that pretended
itself an altar, though it is not.

There's blood, he said
and I am suddenly shooting with pain.
I have been so careful with my dry,
I forgot that water is needed here

so my body offers blood.
He finishes, and there are loose runs
all over my pillowcase,
a trail of pulled silk and ruin.

IN WHICH THE GIRL BECOMES A YOUTUBE CLIP

Whenever these things
happen, my bones turn
so white, it's nearly
blinding. All that
white fire wrapped
in all my black
skin.

                                                &

It's just a dance
because it's just
my body like it's
just a tree despite
the rope but my
graveyard looks
so different from theirs.

&

I watch my professor
stumble right over my
own body cuz I'm so
black and I'm so girl
that it's like I popped
right onto the screen
and stayed there.

                                                &

I know it's my whole
body in that white boy's
mouth when he says
It's so interesting cuz
when all the lights were off
the video started playing
the screen lit my face
and all I felt were teeth.

37

AFTER ST. LOUIS, GOD

octavia butler reminded us that 'god is change.' st. louis is a city overflowing with god. — *Adrienne Maree Brown*

St. Louis is a city
overflowing with
God. St. Louis is a
city overflowing
with hands. St.
Louis is a fist of
a city. God is an
open hand
overflowing. A
hand is a small
city. God is a
city overflowing
with fists.
St. Louis is God
with or without
the open hands,
with or without
the fists.
A city is a fist
overflowing with
God. God is St.
Louis becoming.
God is a city
overflowing with
St. Louis & St.
Louis & St. Louis.
Our hands are all
overflowing with
fists in the shape
of St. Louis. St.
Louis is a city of
after-God. After
God, each fist is

its own city.
Each city
overflows with
or without God.
After God, St.
Louis is a fistful
of open hands.
God is a city
building fists to
protect the hands.
Every city is
overflowing with
fistfuls of St.
Louis. Our hands
are overflowing
with Gods in the
shape of a city.
A city of fists is
still open hands
but is overflowing
with after-God.
God is a fist
overflowing
with St. Louis.
The after-God
overflows in all
our fists. After
St. Louis, every
city is a fist
overflowing.

& after St. Louis, God.

UNBUTTONED & UNBOTHERED: ON IMAGINING THAT FREEDOM PROBABLY FEELS LIKE GETTING *THE ITIS*

Look at our bellies,
peeling open in hunger,
feeding on fliers & bullhorns
& tweets about   *free*
dom   like it's a candlelight
dinner, or a thick outdoor
barbecue with butter &
lawn chairs & scraped knees.
Look at our anxious lips,
the sore hinges of our jaws
clamped around every piece of text,
tonguing each quote in search
of some greens & pig feet.
How the growl in our gut
carries itself across the country,
desperate to feed on   *fre*   *e*
ddd   *om*   like it's full
of black folks, swollen round
with joy & a mouthful of ornaments.
A table full of the kitchen's blessings,
whole bowls of *free   ee   eee   eeee*
steaming under our nose,
drunk with centuries of starving,
now finally feeding on   *f*
reeeeeeeeeeeee   *d*
om   like it's black folks'
bellies stuffed with ENOUGH,
whole bodies celebrating *the itis*,
got our bones dressed in satisfied.
Our ghost uncles & great-great
grand aunts finally draped across
everyone's living room armchair,
unbuttoned & unbothered,

got an armful of finally *fr fffr ffffreee*
filling America's ravenous gut,
putting all the bloodied fields / fists,
all the dripping trees / heels & bridges,
all of them, all those ghosts and
all their glory, all that blood and
all those bodies, finally to sleep.
That's some kind of free.

ACKNOWLEDGMENTS

Grateful acknowledgment is made to the editors of the journals where versions of these poems first appeared:

Connotation Press: "Questions for the Woman I Was Last Night, 1" and "Questions for the Woman I Was Last Night, 3"

Drunk in a Midnight Choir: "Sankofa"

Muzzle Magazine: "Conjuring: A Lesson in Words and Ghosts" and "How America Loves Chicago's Ghosts More Than the People Still Living in the City"

The Offing: "Blood"

Word Riot: "Quentin Tarantino or Why I Do Not Trust You with My History or On Wearing a Gaudy Robe While Grabbing the Ass of a Naked Black Woman for a Magazine"

ABOUT THE AUTHOR

Jacqui Germain is a freelance writer, essayist, Callaloo Fellow and Pushcart Prize nominated poet living in St. Louis, Missouri. Her writing focuses on historical and contemporary iterations of black, brown and indigenous resistance, which she believes is deeply urgent work that both exists on the page and extends beyond it. Jacqui has represented Washington University in St. Louis on the national poetry stage on five separate occasions and was the 2014 Katherine Dunham Fellow with the St. Louis Regional Arts Commission. Her poems have been published or are forthcoming in *Word Riot, The Offing,* and *Muzzle Magazine,* in addition to Sundress Publications' 2015 Best of the Net Anthology.

OTHER BOOKS BY BUTTON POETRY

Aziza Barnes, *me Aunt Jemima and the nailgun.*

J. Scott Brownlee, *Highway or Belief*

Sam Sax, *A Guide to Undressing Your Monsters*

Nate Marshall, *Blood Percussion*

Mahogany L. Browne, *smudge*

Neil Hilborn, *Our Numbered Days*

Sierra DeMulder, *We Slept Here*

Danez Smith, *Black Movie*

Cameron Awkward-Rich, *Transit*